AF447862

Redefining Love

This book is dedicated to both my grandmothers:
Thelma Adishian & Doris Ruiz.
The powerful matriarchs whose love for writing and
literature has shaped my entire world.

Michelle Ruiz

Redefining Love

A COLLECTION OF POEMS ON THE MANY FACES OF LOVE

Copyright © 2023 Michelle Ruiz
First Edition 2023

All rights reserved.
No part of this book may be reproduced or transmitted in any form or by any means, electronic or mechanical, including photocopying, recording or any information storage or retrieval system without permission from the copyright holder.

Publisher: Michelle Ruiz
Editing: Jennifer Cole
Cover image: Adobe Stock Images
Cover design: Book Lingo
Publishing Management: Clare-Rose Julius
Typesetting & eBook Conversion: Book Lingo

Set in 10 point on 15 point Adobe Garamond Pro

ISBN (print):

TABLE OF CONTENTS

CHAPTER THREE: GODDESS LOVE

CHAPTER FOUR: WORLDLY LOVE

INTRODUCTION

I was born and raised in the Bay. I grew up in Castro Valley, California, and made my life-long dream of becoming an English teacher come true at the age of 23 in my very own hometown. Working side by side with many of the teachers that had once taught me left me with a sense of honor. I got into teaching with the mindset of wanting to change and improve the world, and the best way to do so is to inspire our youth to make a difference. I wanted to give back to the community that raised me.

Throughout the years my beloved colleagues and I have organized poetry units and events for students and the community. When I was in middle school, I hated poetry. It felt confusing and antiquated. I didn't begin to grasp the love and appreciation for poetry until attending the required college courses for my English degree. My beloved professor exposed me to diverse and interesting poems that tugged at my heart strings. When I became a teacher, I wanted to cultivate a love for poetry in my students from a much earlier age. The best way to engage middle schoolers is to make the content relatable. I decided to develop a poetry unit that utilized the history and development of hip-hop as an introduction to poetry. The unit begins with a game. The students have to guess whether the quote in the presentation is a hip-hop lyric or a line from a poem. The energy in the class explodes as they try to guess the difference only to realize there is not much difference at all. Hip-hop is poetry, and poetry is everywhere. This activity allows them to see poetry in a different light. By the end of the unit students write and perform an original poem. They then vote on which performances were the most powerful and are given the opportunity to perform their poems in a more public after-school setting.

Poetry has been my lifeline during these challenging years of teaching during a global pandemic. When feeling burnt out and unmotivated I would ask students to give me three words and I would write them a poem. This was a beautiful gift for all of us and inspired me to use poetry as a way to motivate and connect with others. Students' eyes lit up when I turned their words into a poem, and over time I would catch students writing poetry instead of staring at their screens. The beauty of any art form is how contagious it can be.

After spending almost a decade as a middle school teacher I decided to pursue my other dream of becoming a published writer. This book of poetry explores the various forms of love: self-love, romantic-love, feminine-love, and love for the world intertwined with social-emotional themes that promote healthy mindsets. All my life I was exposed to unhealthy love from the media. Love was always about finding Prince Charming, and it took me many years to learn to fall in love with myself. That's where this poetry book starts — with loving ourselves. My purpose was to create a book of poems to inspire people to embrace the various forms of love in an inclusive way. I want to celebrate all the different aspects of life and love, and hope my poems can leave the readers with a sense of contentment and a desire to embrace love in order to make this world a brighter place.

PROLOGUE

Writing poetry in the dark
candles flickering like a work of art,
blood rushing to my foot as it falls asleep.

Trying to find the words
to capture things
I don't quite understand
and yet,
my words always
bring me back to
love.

CHAPTER ONE

SELF-LOVE

1. "Naked"

I've always thought I look
better without any clothes on
Nothing ever seems to fit
as sweetly as the feeling
of my own skin.

2. "Pleasure"

To think we need
another to make love
is madness
in fact, light a candle
and ignite the flame
between your legs.
Sit back and allow
the sensation to rise
and flow from your toes
to your mind.
Unwind.
Kiss your own lips,
dance between sheets,
flee to the heavens,
don't you dare stop.

Gasp for air,
arch your back,
search for the rhythm
to reach completeness
and allow yourself to
release
all
the
things
holding you back
from peace.

3. "Creation (Part I)"

Paper rustling in the wind
as I write down lines
of poetry
that fill me
with harmony,
like the way
piano keys
create a melody
and give me
everything
I'll ever need.

4. "Creation (Part II)"

Ease is reached
when love flows
from our fingertips
into manuscripts
searching
for peace and release
from the memories
sketched into trees
and buried in the roots
of the ones we once were.

5. "Denial"

To love one's self
is an enigma,
like a siren,
or mystery
we may never solve.

Hiding behind
cliffhangers and
masquerade balls,
we create perplexity
and bewilderment;
cages of dismay.

Hate,
an innate ability
to love ourselves
unconditionally
we deny.

But, why?

6. "Extension"

Determined to dream
of resiliency and courage,
when in reality
we sometimes refuse to see
the greatness we seek
is already within
our beating chest.

We must forgive ourselves
for all the times we denied
ourselves a chance to thrive,
to be wild,
to laugh beneath a starlit sky
with other women
who inspire and empower.

Sometimes we must be brave,
and extend our hand
with the same care
we extend to others.

7. "Affirmations"

I am beautiful,
like the thyme that grows
between cobblestones.

I am happy,
like fresh water
after a long run.

I am enough,
like the rocks being
molded by waves.

Simply being,
glistening.

I am me.

8. "My Body"

Curvy and sturdy,
I was built to carry
expectations in my hips,
worries in my ovaries,
and potential in the
tips of my toes.

Does it show?
When I was thirteen
the ache of period pain didn't compare
to the desire to shrink myself year after year
out of fear of that bedroom mirror.

It took thirty years
for me to embrace
the way my thighs kiss,
the way my body folds
and stretches,
the sweet caresses
of my breasts,
the softness
of my skin.

My body an oasis,
a taste of
freedom.

9. "Dreams"

Sometimes she dreams
of planting seeds,
of traveling overseas,
of sipping Italian wine
as fine as pasta dipped
in rich sauces
flavored with possibilities
and opportunities
beyond her wildest dreams.

10. "Italy"

Captivating starlit nights
sipping wine at sunsets
writing poetry at dawn
shutters never drawn,
the rolling hills
serene and picturesque.

Limoncello at lunch,
surrounded by women
sharing stories and intentions
of what this journey shall bring.

Pesto seasoned with cheese
streets bleeding with history.

I've been searching for love
in all the wrong places,
never realizing it's always
been within me.

I have fallen in love
with me
in Italy.

11. "Letting Go"

May you never be afraid
to scrape your knees
from skipping,
or falling
in love with people
who make you feel
peaceful and light,
the ones like the wind
on a summer day
or tea on a winter night.

We spend most our lives
holding back,
pausing,
worrying,
hesitating,
and not enough time playing.

Let go of high expectations,
judgment,
perfectionism,
because life isn't meant
to be stiff or stagnant.

It's meant to be full of action.

Moving forward when we hold
on to what's already gone
is impossible.

Remember, you are powerful.

You are enough.

You have the strength
to let go.

12. "Life"

Death doesn't scare her,
but a life without laughter sure does.

13. "Forgiveness"

I forgive those who have done me wrong
    especially
    the ones
    who promised forever
    when they had hands
    they had not grown into
    yet.

            The ones who
        never called or took the time
        to recognize how their lies
        made me question my own
            abilities.

The ones who commanded space
    in my world,
    only to cancel plans
    and come back again and again,
    only to cancel
    again.

            The ones who put me on display,
          an idolized version
           they conjured
           like a spell
          that stole my magic.

The ones who made me feel small,
    or too much,
    the ones who explained
    at my expense.

            I forgive those who
            have done me wrong.

        Because I've had the power
                all along.

                But first
            I must forgive
                myself.

14. "Hope"

Vulnerability
is a dance of resiliency,
an unyielding demonstration
of hope.

To be
susceptible
to openness
no matter how
many times
the vast ocean
sweeps you under.

To be
brave enough
to fall in love
no matter how
many times pain
has knocked
at your door.

To be vulnerable
is to be human.

It is to have hope.

CHAPTER TWO

ROMANTIC LOVE

1. "Love"

Love is my queen
and I am her faithful servant,
for she promises me a haven
to rest my weary head
whenever I need her.

2. "Safe"

The thickness
of vulnerability
wafts in the air
as she writes love letters that dip
into the inner workings of her soul.

The taste of regret on her lips,
forgiveness caught in her throat
coated with stress.
The essence of love
she fails to understand.

A spring breeze
from the open window eases
the uneasiness beneath her
chest,
and yet,
she can't take her eyes off
the blackberry bush borne with thorns
that keep it safe,
but alone.

3. "First Love"

When I dream of you
it's as if you never left,
and yet you are always leaving.
As if we are tied by past life bonds
roses intertwine, the depth of murky ponds.
Like wild horses running for that last bit of sunlight
time was never on our side.

Acceptance of what is
instead of what's lost
burdens my thoughts
and manifests in dreams
of you and me.

4. "Regrets"

The sword penetrates
her chest
as a vile smile
crosses
his cursed lips.

Stained with promises
dipped in regrets,
but she couldn't see past
his blue eyes.

5. "Broken"

When a boy is broken
his edges can cut a lover wide open
shards of glass in her heart and in her back.
But especially in her mind.
But never all at once.
No, a boy who is broken takes his time
he knows how to survive
how to use a woman to fill the void inside.
Like a heroin addict
he's more concerned with the rush,
the high of all the lies
the women he can conquer and chastise
telling them they are crazy for questioning.
But the thing is, a woman always knows.
From the wife in the attic to Daisy Buchanan
hell hath no fury like a woman scorned.
Doesn't matter how beautiful or talented she may be
Doesn't matter if she's even fucking Beyonce
strong shoulders, or fierce loyalty
doesn't matter if she pays all the bills.
A boy who is broken
doesn't know how to love.
When a boy is broken
he may use his fists as a form of coping,
instead of fighting the emotional demons
he's been ignoring.

Using drugs, sex, and violence
instead of diving into self-reflection and meditation
he will have plenty of excuses and reasons
why he will never be the king you desire
who brings his queen higher.
He may use frivolous words
and make promises he can never keep
He may hold his lover tight and never realize
that women aren't angels of the house
or some silly prize.

We can't fix broken men
we just don't have the time.

I thank God, the universe, or whatever powers there
may be
that I'm able to cut you out like a tumor and be free.
Now that I know the truth and there is undeniable
proof
I can move on and live in peace
knowing no innocent soul is connecting you and me.
Honestly, my broken boy, the first thought that came
to mind
was damn, that baby could have been mine.
Which made me feel nothing but pity
because no woman is deserving
of your toxic excuse of love.
I hope this forces you to grow up
to become the man I thought you could be
so your baby girl can learn that not all men are creeps.

6. "Intoxication"

Intoxicating thoughts,
once meditative mantras
turned into haunting anthems
of handsome lovers
I cannot forgive.

Bombarding memories of
manipulation and deceit
creeping into my dreams,
leaving me thirsty,
preventing
me from ever truly healing.

Addiction like intoxication
infiltrating the bloodstream
due to the media's indoctrination
of princes and saviors
who don't even know
how to save themselves
from intoxicating thoughts.

7. "Dive In"

Sometimes I want to dance
naked under the moon
with as many lovers as there are stars,
to dive into a body of water
so my body invites her
to fill me with femininity and desire.

8. "Disconnect"

She stands in an open field
demanding to feel
the grass
beneath her feet,
instead of the beating
in her chest.

9. "Thirsty"

She's looking for love,
as the tequila begins to flush
her face and slur her words
into a beautiful melody
of thin dreams
peeking above the surface
like crop tops,
or lime on the edge of a cup
just out of reach.

Because most loves
leave her thirsty.

10. "New Beginnings"

Letting go is the
first step
to new adventures
of the heart.

The mind replays
past loss
on repeat
until we realize
nothing
worth seeing
is in the rear view.

11. "Feelings"

When I start catching feelings
the chirping of birds
sound like romantic melodies,
words bloom into poetry,
and laughter
heals old wounds
spilling like
paint on a canvas.

12. "Falling"

Why do I fear greatness?

Why do I keep my -------------- distance

when all I want to do is

    fall

        in love

            with all

                your sounds?

13. "Wonder"

When you
recommend a
romantic movie
to me,
I wonder if you see
me as the
leading lady
in yours.

14. "The Talk"

Lavender blooms
in flower beds,
like romance blooms
between silent glances,
gracing of hands,
noticing the way
their nose crinkles when he laughs,
the nervous laughter
after long discussions
of whether or not
your caterpillar of a romance
is ready to grow
into a butterfly.

15. "Hands"

Hands that melt like sugar,
the lightness of a feather,
bliss and pleasure.

His hands caress my waist
when we interlace
worries are replaced
with the sensation of fingertips on skin.

The feeling when he tightens his grip
around my hips radiates to the tips
of the mountains and the skies.
When I close my eyes
there is the horizon, the sunrise,
the Paris skyline, lips kissed by wine,
as if they were designed to be holding mine.

Hands that melt like sugar,
the lightness of a feather,
bliss and pleasure.

16. "Cherry Trees"

Cherry trees bloom
while you are inside of me.

Legs intertwined like roots
wrapped around power lines,
free from thought or worry,
blooming like morning glory,
electrifying and sublime,
lust drips from your lips
like moonshine.

We've waited so long
denied ourselves a taste
looked but never touched
and now I can't wait
until cherry trees bloom.

17. "Enduring"

The summer breeze
kisses the tops of trees
and I wonder
if he'll be around
when the leaves
begin to fall.

18. "Healthy"

Movies teach us that ropes
are meant to bound the wrists
and necks of lovers,
as if ownership is healthy
and boundaries are bad,
but true love is not
a lyric in a song
or a quote in a movie.

It's about providing peace
and transparency
at you and your lover's will
alone
not creating or falling to demands
or expecting them to understand
what you want
without saying what you want.

It's about holding their hand
in the silence as they process
at their own individual pace.

Love is not a race
nor should it be a carnival ride maybe it's more like a
dip
in the ocean

or a mountain bike ride
terrifying yet serene
as long as we
have been taught to swim
or to ride without training wheels
to communicate
clearly and often
to understand emotional triggers
and not pulling the trigger
when we or our partner
are emotionally volatile
and susceptible to breakdowns and breakups instead
of taking a breath
and counting to ten.

We must realize we are not meant to
save or fix or change
the ones we love.

We do not have scripts
or a dramatic monologue
no chorus or bridge to define us.

We must learn all the things
movies and media never taught us
about love.

19. "Boundaries"

This is the year of creating space
to love you
and me synchronously
by enforcing boundaries
coated in passionate
deliverance like
strawberries
dipped
in chocolate.

20. "Simultaneous"

I love you and me
simultaneously,
in the same way,
we create boundaries
and cultivate vulnerability
like falling in love
while standing on solid ground,
or like the strength of a man
tenderly soothing a newborn
in his calloused hands.

Like the stars shining
and the tides rising,
creating connections and distance
at the same time.

Can't you see?

Everything in the universe
can be
simultaneous.

21. "Like Home"

Wait for a love who makes you feel at home
a love like the heat of turning on a stove
or fresh water straight from the garden hose
on a summer day when you feel most comfortable
without any clothes.
Wait for a love who makes you feel at home.

CHAPTER THREE

GODDESS LOVE

1. "Femininity"

The tenacity
of femininity
grows beyond
time and space.

She is constantly
growing,
because her body
was designed for
nurturing.

Wide hips,
soft belly,
full thighs

the shape of goddesses
who caress and express
the tenacity of femininity.

2. "Rain"

Rain kisses my hair,
and I swear I'll never find despair
as she taps on my window.

The damp soil in my garden
reminds me of the flowers growing from within
blooming, reaching, teaching me to
embrace feminine energy the same way I do the rain.

My body quivers with desire
as I stand outside, barefoot, without my coat
erect and wet,
but I cannot curse the rain
for she is everything.

3. "Strength"

May the boldness
that runs through her veins
never dissipate,
may her appetite for braveness
never falter or halt.

For it's not her fault
the world isn't ready
for someone as bold
as her.

4. "Dance"

I want girls to never wait
to be asked
to dance
backs against the wall
or home alone
without a date.

I want girls to spread
their arms like wings
and spin
to take their hearts
from their beating chests
and raise them
above their heads
like warriors

because girls don't need boys
to dance.

5. "Freedom"

Could you imagine a world
　　　where women walk
　　　　　outside
　　　　　　　alone
　　　　　　　without fear?

Where we grip
dreams instead of keys and
hope instead of mace,
chase chances,
take risks,
fill our pockets
with potential.

　　　A world where we feel
　　　free.

6. "Nurture"

Wrapped up in soft blankets
with the smell of sweet baby
cuddles,
warmth and smiles,
his love is undeniable.

Two queens to serve,
his love unyielding and nurturing
like the earth.

7. "Evasion"

The silk
on her skin
is delicate
decadent
affectionate.

Unwelcome
and weary
of violent invasions
of men,
who silence
her feminine nature.

Like erosion
or poison
her mind is adrift.

Chapped lips,
like a ship
without an
anchor,
waiting
for the captain
to give his orders.

8. "Awakening"

The thrill of the ocean
fills her with clandestine.

An awakening
of desire burns
beneath her chest,
a lover teaches
her the taste of
freedom.

Her soul unrest,
a universal lust
spanning across centuries,
awakening the curiosity
of a young woman
reading the pages
of her story for the first time.

9. "Finesse"

Her finesse
dances with elegance
across the wood floor,
igniting
like a match
on a dragon's breath.

Looking to bury
the flames that beat beneath
her chest
she finds herself
staring into the night air
scared of the fire
just below the surface.

10. "Intention"

With the intention of creation
she holds the camera
with satisfaction,
capturing a moment
of connection
between women
seasoned with adventure,
sipping on wine,
bread dipped in olive oil,
honored by the soil
that birthed so many artists
before them.

All with a desire
to communicate dreams
through the precious act
of writing.

11. "Ancestral"

The spicy earthy aroma
of cardamom
and tiger balm
remind her of her
grandmother.

Long floral skirts
and bangles on her wrists
as she cooks
with the same look
she gives when she's
praying.

Memories as rich
as winning the lottery
like touching grandma's wrist
for wealth and prosperity
like hairspray
that holds these smells
and sounds in place.

She can never escape
the strength of the women
who came before her.

Nor would she ever
want to.

12. "Legacy"

An Ethiopian queen
with the power of her people
running through her veins
reminding her that things
like sorrow and pain
cannot touch
her throne.

Royal blood,
head up
my love,
you are made of
gold.

13. "Admiration"

The muse hits her like a groovy tune,
like the 60's, like an airstream,
like a fixation she can't kick.

A leaf falls from the tree
as she leaves.

She sees how free she can be,
painting murals,
wearing pearls,
shining like the women
she sees on the movie screen.

She is you, and she is me.

14. "Modern Dreams"

Searching for
shades of purple
in her dreams,
lavender helps her sleep
when the brightness
of her screen
screams for
more.

Pouring out her heart
like a cup of tea,
she embraces
the rain,
heart racing,
dancing,
dreams of
romancing.

She falls asleep
remembering life is felt,
not seen on a
screen.

15. "The Land"

Snowfall.

Like a familiar hum
you know by heart,
like the taste of a lover
lingering on your lips,
like wine,
like him
staining the tips
of your memories
with the rhythm of waves,
like warm coffee mugs,
or the blankets wrapped around your legs.

Snowfall reminds us
that ice is meant to melt,
and bind us.

Reminds you of the divine,
how you were raised by praise grass
and sunshine.

16. "Contradicts"

Charismatic
and fair
always willing
to put others first
even when she thirsts
for something deeper,
more sincere,
precious,
and rare.

Water absorbs into air
but it's hard not to stare
and see
how different
she can be.

When she's left
alone
flooded with emotions
that contradict
the air
she breathes.

17. "Vibrancy"

Complacency holds no place
in her vibrant world.

Laughter as flashy as leather pants,
she was born to impact,
to inspire,
to initiate change.

Her world is full of color,
of fabrics,
of painted lips,
of tips and tricks.

Like a queen
she knows
style is everything.

18. "Thriving"

She's graceful and glamorous,
with her warmth and her words.

Unchained from men
who dimmed her style,
bruises and scars
that go beyond the surface.

She's wild and adventurous.

Finally free from controlling egos
who couldn't see
she never needed a man
to empower her,
for her power
has always been within.

Waiting to strike
like a Venus flytrap,
a lioness, or a fierce empress,
she prepares to take flight
through healing
and writing,
to create a life
of adventure worth reading.

19. "Patience"

Happiness like a serene
painting.

The shades of the lake
blend together with such beauty.

She paints
with an eye
that sees why
patience and design
intertwine.

20. "Light"

She's calling in light
like a crocodile calling
in their prey.

Rising from the surface,
she opens her mind
to ancient tenacity
passed down from generations
of fearless crocodiles
refusing to release the strength
of their teeth
no matter how
murky the water gets.

21. "Aging"

Her eyes hold decades
of experiences
as fragile as blue tulips,
and as grand as mountains.

Language is her world
and aging is on her mind,
but nothing creates grace like time.

Her spirit is strong,
balance is key,
a life of activism,
of learning,
of dedication to family
lands on her shoulders.
Travel rests on her hips,
stories on her lips.

Being in her presence
is a gift,
a constant and swift
reminder that age
doesn't define us,
but we are shaped
by experiences
held in the wise eyes
of women just like her.

22. "Voices"

Gratitude sparkles in her tears
as she finds the courage
to speak her truth.

The truth is,
in the land of the free
freedom doesn't come easy.

She comes from a long line
of warriors,
women like mighty buffalo
who thrive in collaborative communities
and dismantle toxic hierarchies,
whose battle cries
scream of equality.

With skin as gorgeous as the night
they raise their voices to fight
white supremacy and the chokehold
it has on our freedom.

See, she is gifted by the ancestral
strength of those who fought before
to change the narrative
by dancing with judges
and sharing her story

in a room full of white faces,
women who must face
the battle with her.
Side by side,
because this is war
for freedom
and it's time to speak up.

CHAPTER FOUR

WORLDLY
LOVE

1. "Red"

The color that runs through our veins
that unifies us and breaks our chains.
Like blood on a knife
or between a women's thighs.

Red like sacrifice, like Jesus Christ.
Blood like the Stonewall riots.

People bleeding in the streets,
sick and tired of avoiding the police
for simply trying to be
free from bigotry, free from hate.

Freedom like our right to bear arms
to arm neighborhoods against boys
like Trayvon Martin
Boys like Emmett Till whose body
was found bloated and still.

Boys, like Peter Pan, who will never grow up who were
born beautiful and black, but never stood a chance.

If there is no justice there can never be peace.

Red, the symbol of luck, joy, and happiness
for Chinese citizens who left everything
to build the first Transcontinental railroad.

Blood pouring into American soil,
to connect and spread trade with ease
Chinese immigrants sacrificed their lives only to be
excluded from naturalization,
equal opportunity, and basic human rights.

Blood like the bond that connects mother to child,
the bond broken at the border
with children in cages
it reminds us of the New Order.

Red like the flag that flew over Auschwitz.

The world screamed never again,
while we caged Japanese Americans.
Red like Washington Redskins.
Red like assimilation.

Red like the bodies of children buried
behind boarding schools
that we never read about in our history books
collecting dust on the shelf.

And many of us sit still when we see
history repeat itself.

Red, the color that ignites the bull,
the color of lust and love.
The color that binds us.

Red is the color of life.

2. "History"

Riots coated
in blood.

The lifeline of
art.

The sounds
of Harlem
or hip-hop
remind us our
struggles are
not new.

3. "Mass Shootings"

Pricked by thorns
when we put on our
rose-colored glasses
and stare into the mirror,
as if mirroring thoughts
and prayers
are just and fair
to prevent the horror
of gunshots echoing in halls.

With blood on our hands
and children's screams ringing
in our ears,
we just stare in the mirror
praying for a clear answer
to end the bloodshed,
not seeing the answer is with
you and it's with me.

4. "White Supremacy"

The thing about
white supremacy
is that it feeds off apathy,

an insidious monster
that fears common sense
or any sense of compassion.

It keeps us caged
by complacency,
never realizing
the abundance
that awaits

once we slay
white supremacy.

5. "Listen to Maya Angelou"

Maya Angelou spoke of the caged bird.
It sings of freedom, she said.

Freedom.

Not white picket fences
that fence white people in
affluent neighborhoods
with high-performing schools,
farmers markets and Whole Foods.

No, the caged bird sings of freedom.

Freedom from institutionalized hate.
The ability to choose your own faith.
To escape the heteronormative ideal mate.
So many of us are caged.

Trapped behind gender norms
or this intrinsic need to perform
better, faster, stronger.
Enslaved to Capitalism
or this dream of wanting more.
Roosevelt said, "comparison is the thief of joy"
But, comparison is also the jailer.

He keeps us depressed,
and dreaming of greener grass.
So much water and fertilizer to keep up the mask.
If only we appreciated native plants.

But, nah.
We praise colonization, dehumanization.
Caged by corporations
who target and exploit us,
who poison our water,
murder our fathers,
brainwash us into dependence
and threaten to leave if we fight or restrict them.

It's silly to think we are truly free.
But the thing is, not all of our cages are the same.
Let's start with me:
Being a young, white woman
would a police officer fire his gun
if I reached into my purse?
Would he throw me to the ground or worse?
Would I ever be asked where I'm from?
To go back to where I belong?
It's wrong, but not all cages are created equal.

Do Chinese, Japanese, Vietnamese, Korean, Indian
American children see themselves represented on the
big screen?

Do people with disabilities truly
feel understood and seen?

Can a transgender person use a bathroom without
fear in their own workspace?

Does a man fear running alone after dark without
mace?

Maya Angelou spoke of the caged bird
It sings of freedom, she said.

Freedom.

It's about time we actually listened.

6. "Purple"

The color of the soul,
the part of us we spend so much time searching for.
Like ghost stories told by candlelight,
or packing our bags and taking flight
to awaken our spirit, to lift our consciousness to
greater heights.

Buddhism believes the breath connects and binds us,
like learning to meditate in India on rooftops.
Like Namaste at the end of Hot Box Yoga,
or closing your eyes and listening to Nirvana,
meditation finds each of us differently, speaks to us
uniquely.

Sometimes we don't trust what we don't understand.
Holy Wars feel like a contradiction,
yet religion and war seem to go hand in hand.
Surrounded by pain and destruction,
soldiers' souls die on the front lines
and return home shattered like coal mines.
Purple hearts pinned to military collars
to represent the sacrifice and the honor.

So many vets turn purple
from the cold of the city streets
homeless, honorable, not looking for pity,
but to be treated humanely.

Purple like the color of bruises
that appear on battered skin.
Women who are strong and resilient.

Purple like the fighter with a fire in his eyes,
every punch a release for the demons he keeps inside.
Trying to fight his father's fists
and the screams of his mother that kept him up at
night.
Purple like the mighty peacock
a symbol of royalty engraved on Persian thrones.

Purple like lavender
healing and relaxing
that treats anxiety, insomnia, and depression.
So many of us inherit trauma in our genes.
From slavery to genocides, trauma marks our soul and
reminds us
that developing your spirit takes practice, and it takes
time.

When you accept Jesus in your heart
but turn your back on people in the streets
it perpetuates the cycle of confusion and despair.
It doesn't matter what you believe, we have to do what
is fair.

Purple like Ursula, who stole souls to grant wishes.
Like airports openly profiling Muslims as terrorists,
or parents forcing children into conversion therapy
supported by our Vice President.

The United States can be awfully villainous.

The president holding up a bible for publicity,
so many Americans stay silent with complicity
when he continues to divide this country
by reducing people to liberals or conservatives.
I wish that everyone knew
our spirit is not red nor is it blue,
we are all connected.

Purple is the heart of our essence
that pushes us beyond our basic needs,
because we know the universe is greater than it
seems.

> **Purple, the color of our spirit
> that drives us to serve others.**

> **Purple.**

7. "Intuition"

Intuition
like a mist,
a whisper,
a butterfly kiss.

It speaks of wishes,
of risks, of winds
in the distance.

It finds us in the silence,
when the lenses
of our glasses break.

Shards of glass
paint the path,
waves and artificial light
bombard our senses.
Always distracted.

Manifesting desires
like a fire kindling,
we hear it in the
crackling of wood,
the screams of thunder,
and wonder
if our voices
are clear.

8. "Grind"

Lace paints the wide
space with intricate designs
of our worried minds
that bind us to an
unbearable grind.

9. "Masculinity"

Masculinity is a web
of power and fragility.

It's the complex
understanding
of mind and feelings.

It's about confidence
and escaping the narrow definition
created by centuries
of waves being beaten against rocks,

It's about time we
redefine masculinity.

10. "Beauty of the Non-Binary"

The bliss of
existence
exists on a
spectrum
of hopes and fears.

It is about
the presence
of nature
who presents
the beauty
and diversity
of fungi and frogs.

The bliss of
existence
is about love
free from labels
meant to divide
and conquer,

The bliss of
existences
is for
everyone.

11. "Blue"

The sound of waves crashing against rocks,
raindrops on a roof,
or when the violin makes love to the harp
creating a harmonious symphony
that involves understanding and being in sync.
NSYNC like Justin, Joey, JC, Lance and Chris.
Like paint coming together on a canvas
creating the blue sky with broad strokes,
meeting the depths of the sea with the artist's hopes
and dreams of creating a piece that is harmonious and
free.
Each detail unique, needed, and appreciated.
Blue, the color of harmony.
Like the melting pot of people coming together
earnestly,
each culture recognized and accepted, truly a blessing
to live, and work, and dream in the United States.
Blue, the color of the sky,
So many Americans reach so high,
only to realize their boots never had straps
and the melting pot was left on the stove far too long.
People feeling burnt out waiting for that harmonious
song
they were promised as kids when we stood tall and
strong.
Blue like the color of police
protectors, heroes, and keepers of peace.

A few bad apples, they say.
But a few bad apples can ruin the rest,
especially when our scales are out of balance.
Like an old man being pushed in the street
or restricting a man's ability to breathe
or refusing to arrest the men who killed Breonna
Taylor in her sleep.
A knee like a noose, a gun like a whip.
Blue lives can't matter when they act as slave masters.
Blue like balance,
like a waitress wearing a mask as she does a
complicated dance,
like in Bachata when two partners move with
harmonious romance.
Harmony needs rhythm and soul
like the Harlem Renaissance or the Queen of Rock n
Roll.
Like closing your eyes and waiting for that beat to
drop.
Harmony takes years of practice and discourse
to put humanity on the correct course.
Blue like unity.
In 2015 all 50 states legalized gay marriage.
In 2010 "Don't ask, don't tell" is repelled
so men and women can serve this country
no matter who the hell they were born to love.
From James Baldwin to Taylor Swift,
social justice is meant to shift
us from drunk karaoke to a beautiful symphony.

> *Blue like humanity and equality*
> *which is the only way to reach perfect harmony.*

12. "Guide"

The raven kisses the night sky
and reminds us of why
we must trust the stars
to guide
us.

He sings of truth and desire,
of spiritual fire,
of connection and wit,
of hope within darkness.

13. "Violent Fruit"

The melancholy
melody
plays quietly
for the ones
we've forgotten.

We light a candle,
say a prayer,
and continue to eat
the rotten fruit
we always have.

Change comes in waves,
and if we aren't careful
the undertow
will submit us
to her will.

14. "Silence"

Silence provides a stillness
to witness
light and darkness,
to savor
the flavor of sweetness,
the creaminess of dreams unseen.
Like the smell of pine
and burning forward
from your childhood.

The sacredness of communication
buried beneath your skin
begins to process in the silence,
and reminds you to speak up
when the wool on your skin
feels like too much.

Silence,
our most cherished friend.

15. "Green"

The color of nature
like the tip of a glacier or legislature
to protect our planet
from the bandits
in their tall steel towers breaking the balance
of mother nature's beautiful dance.

Green like fawns frolicking in grass
or green leaves kissing our cheeks
as we listen to nature speak
from chirping to water flowing.
Green like redwoods growing
in soil so precious and ancient.

Dakota Access Pipeline protests
oil poisoning like fish trapped in nets
Why do we refuse to listen and continue to disrespect
the Lorax who speaks for the trees?
Do we want a world like WALL-E,
fat and disconnected, floating through space?
Listen to the children, they can't afford to wait
The effects of climate change are what their
generation will have to face.

Increase in disease, polluted air to breathe
Sea levels are rising and coral is bleaching
We need to turn to our children for teaching.

Greta Thunberg sailed on a boat and spoke,
but she's not the only one.
Mari Copeny wrote to the president in 2016
explaining the water in Flint, Michigan wasn't clean
which is an excellent example of
environmental racism
According to the census Flint is over 50% black
and half of the residents live below the poverty line.
Many communities of color are targeted or neglected.
The poorest people suffer from natural disasters
With sea levels rising that means there is more
likelihood of flooding
when many people are already drowning
from bills, from fear, from inequalities
Clean drinking water is a right we shouldn't have to
fight for,
but our clean water is shrinking, and our air quality is
decreasing
Our cancer rates are rising, and it isn't surprising.
Green is the color of nature, the color of motherhood
nature is where we get our water, our nurture, our
food.

But cramming hundreds of chickens in a cage is not
natural or good,
it is a breeding ground for pain and disease.
Some communities have no access to fresh fruit or
groceries
and are forced to feed their children fast food that is
processed.

So many communities are starving, so many animals
are dying.
Mother nature was set on fire with the industrial
revolution
There is no mistake or confusion, mother nature is
crying.

Green, like a boy's ability to fall in love with another
boy
it is always natural to love and to seek joy.
Mother nature opens her arms to accept everyone the
way they are.
Nature endures and grows
Flowers always bloom in the spring, even after the
heaviest of snows.
Every winter deer shed their antlers,
like snakes shed their skin
like lionesses protecting their prides and kin,
or a wolf tenderly cleaning her pup's fur.

> **Green is the color of nature;**
> **she will help us if we let her.**

16. "Abandonment"

When we abandon
the dance of nature
we abandon ourselves,
for nature
moves to the rhythm
of waves,
dips into sunshine,
and caresses their partner
with the dignity
of an olive tree
growing in Tuscany.

17. "Weeds"

Thousands of yellow plants paint my backyard
Bright and beautiful
they reach for the sun,
border the beach where the joggers run
They dance in the wind
prance and pretend.

At first glance they seem to ascend
as royal kings and queens of the flower kingdom
but they do not live in a golden tower
nor do they drink the delectable nectar
No, they are nothing but a weed.

Beautiful but unwanted
small but mighty
vigorously growing wherever they please
the little yellow weeds.

18. "Integrity"

Sifting through litter
that floats to the surface,
buoyant and bold,
worthless.

Searching for integrity
as the world unfolds.
The preposterous notion
of decency,
is so far and few
between.

From garbage islands
to depletion of the o-zone,
it's as if we don't
owe
anyone
anything.

Integrity
lost at sea.

19. "Slow Down"

Nature's patience

in essence

enlightens us,

brightens us,

gives us reasons

to slow down.

www.ingramcontent.com/pod-product-compliance
Lightning Source LLC
Chambersburg PA
CBHW051439140726
47987CB00006B/2447